HYPNOTISM

HYPNOTISM
Hocus Pocus or Science?

by Vivian Kirby
ILLUSTRATED WITH PHOTOGRAPHS

JULIAN MESSNER
NEW YORK

Design by Beverly Haw Leung, A Good Thing, Inc.

Library of Congress Cataloging in Publication Data

Kirby, Vivian.
    Hypnotism : hocus pocus or science?

    Bibliography: p.
    Includes index.
    1. Hypnotism—Juvenile literature.   2. Hypnotism—
Therapeutic use—Juvenile literature.   I. Title.
BF1141.K5   1985   154.7   84-29484
ISBN 0-671-45802-7

This one is for
Kathleen

Acknowledgements

Many thanks to the following individuals for reviewing and otherwise assisting with the sections of this book pertinent to their expertise.

Gail Blackwell, Alpha Hypnosis, Ltd.

Gil Boyne, Hypnotism Training Institute of Los Angeles

Richard S. Broughton, Ph.D., Foundation for Research on the Nature of Man, The Institute for Parapsychology

Ruth Fitzgerald, D.D.S.

Jack Houck

Mary Kay Wright-Malear, John F. Kennedy University

Photo Credits

Ruth Fitzgerald, D.D.S., pp. 37, 38, 39.
Foundation for Research on the Nature of Man, The Institute for Parapsychology, pp. 62, 66.
Jack Houck, p. 69.
Library of Congress, pp. 11, 48.
Sharon A. Martin, p. 42.
Doug McFadden, Alpha Hypnosis Clinics International, pp. 22, 24, 25.
Ormond McGill, pp. 46, 47, 52, 53.
National Library of Medicine, pp. 12, 13, 16, 28.
All other photos are the author's.

Contents

Evil hypnotist influences beautiful girl in this old engraving.

1

Witchcraft
or
Science?

Sinister shadows dance on the walls of a gloomy room. A pretty girl stares helplessly at the flickering flame of a candle held in the hand of an evil-looking man. The man chants, "Your eyes are growing heavy and you are sleepy ... very, very sleepy. Now you are in my power. When I snap my fingers you will open your eyes, walk out to the cliff, and step off into the ocean."

The snap of his fingers sounds like a gunshot. The victim slowly opens her eyes, stands up, and walks with robotlike steps into the dark and windy night. She moves slowly toward the cliff's edge, pauses, then plunges into the ocean hundreds of feet below.

A scene like this is what many people imagine when they hear the word "hypnosis." They think of it as hocus-pocus magic, or trickery. That's because most people know very little about hypnosis. They only know what they've read in stories or seen in horror movies.

Yet hypnosis has probably been practiced since the beginning of humankind. In ancient times, priests and priestesses went into trances to predict the future. They claimed to talk to the gods or to the dead. Witch doctors and shamans or medicine men could put whole groups of people into trances with their hypnotic dancing, chanting, and shaking of magic rattles. Sometimes they healed the sick, and sometimes their powers of suggestion could make healthy people die. Even today, shamans perform the ancient rituals involving hypnotism in certain parts of the world. Ancient Egyptian doctors did delicate surgery without anesthetics. How did they stop pain so they could operate? They probably used a form of hypnosis.

The skills of the ancient doctors, priests and sorcerers were closely guarded secrets for many centuries. Then, in the 1700s, an Austrian named Franz Anton Mesmer decided to expose those secrets to scientific study.

Mesmer decided that an invisible force tied everything and everyone in the universe together. He called this force the "Universal Fluid." He believed that when a person's universal fluid was balanced, the person was healthy. A person was sick when the universal fluid was out of balance. Mesmer believed that magnets had the power to put the fluid in balance.

Mesmer cured many people with magnets and became famous. In Paris, France, so many people came to him for treatment that he could not see them one at a time. So he filled a large wooden tub with water, glass, and flakes of iron.

An old photograph showing an Indian fakir relaxing on a bed of spikes — he has hypnotized himself so that he feels no pain.

Franz Anton Mesmer

He magnetized the iron, put a lid on the tub, and stuck metal rods through its top. This contraption was called a baquet (bah-KAY), French for bucket. Patients held onto the metal rods of the bacquet as they listened to soft music. After a while, Mesmer would come in and exclaim, "Be healed!" As soon as he would speak, his patients either went limp or began to flop around on the floor. When, a few minutes later, they were back to normal, they seemed to be cured. In this way, Mesmer treated everything from headaches to tumors.

Soon Mesmer decided he did not need the baquet or the magnets. He realized that his patients were cured only after *he* entered the room. Mesmer decided that the healing power belonged to the magnetizer. It flowed from him—through the eyes or the fingertips—into the patient.

Some doctors in Mesmer's lifetime called his cures trickery. Nevertheless, Mesmer was a popular healer, so popular that the king of France decided to investigate his powers. The king sent a group of wise and respected men to watch Mesmer and learn about his cures. Benjamin Franklin, then United States ambassador to France, was a member of that group. The group decided that magnetism had nothing to do with the cures, but that the cures were all in the imagination of the patients. The patients *expected* to have violent physical

Mesmer's baquet.

reactions when Mesmer spoke, and they *knew* they would then be cured.

In those days, however, doctors were trying to shed the image that clung to them of magic and sorcery. They believed only in things that could be seen or felt. Mesmer's universal fluid was invisible, so scientists said it didn't exist. *Mesmerism*, as Ben Franklin's group called it, was pure imagination. So mesmerism faded from popularity. Doctors took over the curing of sickness, and mesmerism was practiced mostly on the stage.

In the mid-1800s, a British doctor named James Braid watched a stage performance of mesmerism. He told his wife about it, calling it all a hoax. Dr. Braid imitated the performance, using his wife as a subject. He probably wanted to show her how foolish it all was. But she promptly went into a deep trance.

Dr. Braid was fascinated and tried his mesmerizing powers on others. He discovered that a person in such a trance felt no pain and seemed sound asleep. Its use for relieving the pain of an operation in those days before anesthesia seemed God-given. Braid called this deep trance *hypnosis*, a word that came from the Greek word "hypnos," which means sleep. As time passed, the word "hypnosis" came to mean the act of leading a person into a trance.

Hypnosis became popular with doctors again and was used in operating rooms for several years. Unfortunately, it took a long time to hypnotize a scared patient. Hypnotism did not always work: not everyone could be hypnotized. But until science discovered chemicals that would quickly put anyone to sleep, hypnosis was better than nothing at all.

Doctors in different countries kept on using hypnotism to treat patients. They learned that there were many kinds of hypnotic trances. Some were so light that a soft but unexpected noise would bring a patient out of the hypnotized state. Others were so deep that the patient seemed unconscious. These doctors also learned that talking to people while they were hypnotized seemed to effect cures faster. They got some surprises as well. One doctor was astounded when a hypnotized patient told him exactly what his problem was and how it should be cured. Except under hypnosis, this patient knew nothing of medicine.

Many doctors studied hypnosis. Sigmund Freud, the great founder of psychoanalytic treatment of emotional disorders, was among them. But Freud was not good at it and stopped using hypnosis after a very short time.

Writers also became interested in hypnotism in the 1800s. Unfortunately, they always seemed to give the power of hypnotism to their villains. George du Maurier's book, *Trilby*, is probably the best known on the subject. It is about an evil man named Svengali who mesmerizes a young girl named Trilby. He makes her into a great singer, but she can sing only when she is hypnotized. Trilby makes a fortune with her singing but doesn't know it. Svengali steals her money and also her soul. Toward the end of the story, Svengali is killed. Since he owns Trilby's soul, she cannot live without him and she, too, dies. The illustration on page 8 is from the original book.

Trilby is still read today, and it has been made into several movies. Many people believe the part about hypnotism. This story and others have helped to keep alive the feeling that hypnotism is black magic.

After World Wars I and II, many soldiers couldn't forget how horrible war had been. They were haunted by their memories. It was found that hypnotism could help these ex-soldiers to either forget or to accept the past and look to the future. This helped to renew scientific interest in hypnotism.

Some doctors in World War I treated patients with hypnosis.

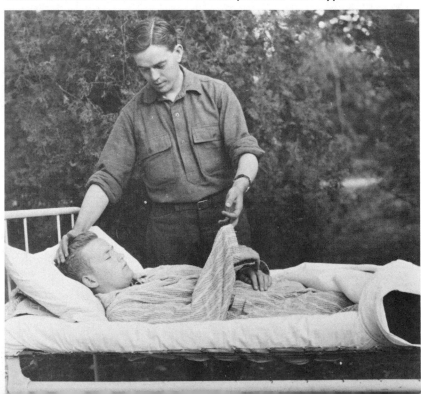

Then, in 1956, a book called *The Search for Bridey Murphey* was published in the United States. The author told a lot about hypnosis and of how he came to learn and study it. Then he told of a woman who, while hypnotized, remembered a previous lifetime. This theme of reincarnation—being born again—caused many people to speak against the book. Once again, hypnotism was called black magic, witchcraft. Even today, the laws of some states lump witchcraft and hypnotism together and outlaw both.

Scientists, however, continued to study the many uses for hypnotism. In 1958, the Council on Mental Health of the American Medical Association said that hypnosis was real, and useful for treating some health problems. In 1961, the American Psychiatric Association also accepted hypnosis. A long history of amazing cures finally convinced many physicians that hypnosis was neither magic nor witchcraft, but rather, a remarkable medical tool.

So why do writers still write stories about evil hypnotists who take control of their victims and make them do terrible things like walk off cliffs? Because it makes an exciting story!

Hypnosis Today

If hypnosis is neither magic nor witchcraft, what is it?

The words used to describe hypnosis have changed over the years. Many years ago, the term "trance" was used, only to be replaced later by "mesmerism." The word "hypnosis" followed and more recently the term "altered state of consciousness" took its place. Only the names change. The state they describe remains the same.

Many people think that being in a hypnotized state is like being asleep. Even the dictionary calls hypnosis "a sleeplike state." But "sleeplike" only tells how a hypnotized person sometimes looks to others, not about how a hypnotized person thinks and feels. "Altered state of consciousness" comes closer to telling what hypnosis feels like. A hypnotized person is not asleep. In sleep we don't know what's going on around us. People in hypnosis are aware of everything going on around them. It just isn't important to them at the moment.

But what *is* hypnosis? No one really knows for sure. This may sound surprising. Hypnotism obviously works in the brain, and doctors and other scientists know a lot about the brain. They know that our minds function on a conscious and a subconscious level and that each level has its own job to do.

The *conscious* is our thinking mind. With it, we read and write and decide to do all sorts of things. When we're asked a question, we use our conscious mind to think of the answer.

The *subconscious* mind is still something of a mystery. Some experts believe that the subconscious is a memory bank. They believe it remembers details of things we've seen, heard, felt, smelled, tasted or done. Our dreams come from our subconscious. Some people believe that what many call a "soul" is a part of the subconscious mind. Hypnotism is a way of contacting the subconscious.

Most of the time, the information in our subconscious mind is locked away from us. Hypnotism may unlock it. Mike, for example, is terrified of the water. Most of the time he stays away from it, but he feels left out when his friends go swimming and water skiing. Mike tells himself that he must learn to swim. The problem is that he can't. Whenever he steps into anything bigger than a bathtub his throat closes up. It feels as if a monster is choking him. He has to gasp for air. The only way he can breathe freely is to get completely away from the water. He doesn't understand why he's so afraid of something that all his friends take for granted.

Oh, he's heard the story of how he fell into a wading pool when he was a baby and nearly drowned. But Mike's conscious mind knows he couldn't drown in a wading pool, so he doesn't think this experience really has anything to do with his terror. He just knows that if he goes out in a boat or tries to learn to swim, something terrible will happen to him.

Mike's parents want to help. They think hypnosis might be the answer and they search for a skilled, qualified *hypnotherapist*, one who treats with hypnosis. Mike's parents call the local medical and psychological societies for referrals. They learn that there is a Society of Clinical and Experimental Hypnosis and an American Society for Clinical Hypnosis that train hypnotherapists and can make referrals. Mike's parents interview several hypnotherapists, and finally choose one they think will be to Mike's liking.

Meanwhile, Mike wonders what hypnosis will feel like. As a matter of fact, it feels almost like being awake.

Have you ever suddenly caught yourself daydreaming? You're sitting in class with all the other kids, the teacher is talking, but you're bored. You start thinking about something else and soon you feel as if you're a hundred miles away. You know you're still in class, but the class is not important, somehow. Neither are the other kids and neither is the teacher. You simply don't think about them for a while—until an angry voice snaps your name and you're brought back to the classroom with a start.

Or have you ever watched a terrific movie? The theater and all the people around faded as the music led you right into the movie. The villain chased you. You became the hero or heroine. At the end of the movie, it was almost a surprise to find yourself back in the theater with your friends.

Or have you read a book and felt your heart beating faster and faster as the hero's problems plunged from bad to hopeless? Have you cried with the hero when everyone believed the villain's lies? Have you laughed when the villain was caught in his or her own trap? Did the pages of the book seem to turn by themselves right up until the last?

Hypnosis is like this. It is total concentration. For the moment you're concentrating your whole self on only one thing. And hypnosis can be ended just as easily as when your concentration was broken by the teacher calling on you, or the theater lights going up, or the book ending. Most people don't

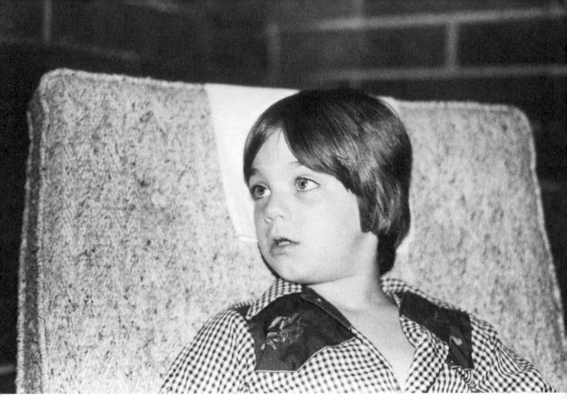

Eyes open in hypnosis have the same far-away look as in daydreaming.

want to believe that hypnosis is so ordinary. It's more exciting to think of it as dangerous and mysterious.

Most experts agree that nearly everyone can be at least partially hypnotized or put into what is called a light trance. The catch is that people in a light trance often think they aren't really hypnotized. They think they're just "going along" with the hypnotist. They think they could open their eyes if they really wanted to. They're partly right. They are cooperating with the hypnotist, and can open their eyes if they want to. They're also hypnotized.

But experts disagree on how deep a state of hypnosis can be achieved the first time someone visits a hypnotherapist. Some experts claim they can lead anyone into a very deep trance the very first time he or she is hypnotized. Others are happy to have their clients reach a light trance the first time. The skill and expectations of the hypnotherapist are important to success. The client must also like and trust the hypnotherapist. Otherwise, regardless of the hypnotherapist's skill, the client's subconscious resistance will prevent a trance, whether deep or light.

Mike is a little frightened, but when he is called into the hypnotherapist's office he takes an instant liking to Dr. Bell. She has a nice smile and her eyes aren't "weird." Dr. Bell explains some facts about hypnosis, first telling Mike that he will be in charge of his own hypnosis. Dr. Bell has no special powers. She will only act as a guide. If Mike chooses to do so, he'll be able to end his hypnosis instantly.

Mike is fairly smart, one of the things that will help him to go into hypnosis. Dr. Bell tells Mike that it's a little harder for men than women to enter hypnosis. She adds that young people between the ages of about six and sixteen are often better subjects than adults. Kids are usually more suggestible, more open to new ideas. That can be good. We have to be suggestible in order to learn new things, and we also have to be imaginative, to think, and to concentrate. Kids think and concentrate all day long, both in and out of school.

Mike still worries that maybe he can't be hypnotized. Dr. Bell says he can, if he's really willing. Willingness is the key word. A person who absolutely doesn't want to be hypnotized usually can't be. The hypnotherapist can't force someone's mind into hypnosis any more than someone can make you like something you really hate.

It's vital to like and trust the hypnotist — and liking and trust show clearly in this young man's face.

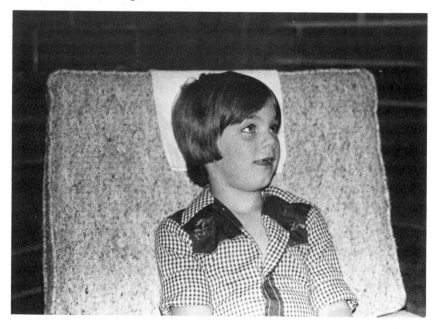

Mike relaxes. His questions are answered, and he is ready to let Dr. Bell hypnotize him. In hypnosis, Mike's conscious mind takes a rest and his subconscious mind responds. He remembers the terror, the choking pain, the fearful attempts to breathe when he nearly drowned. Mike's subconscious also remembers how good it felt to be pulled free and to be able, finally, to breathe. It remembers who pulled him from the water and what that person said and did. Mike's subconscious

Now he appears to be asleep, but his face shows that he is listening to the suggestions of the hypnotist.

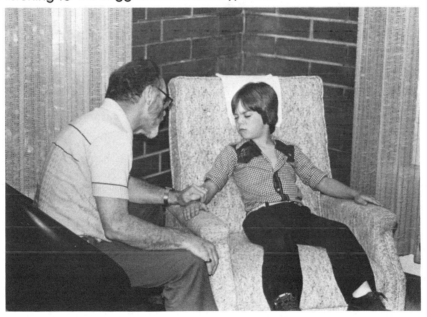

mind also resolved to keep him away from the water from then on. That way, the water could never hurt him again.

With Dr. Bell's help, Mike convinces his subconscious mind that he can't avoid the water forever. He's bigger and stronger now. Once he learns to swim he'll be able to protect himself while he's in the water. When he leaves Dr. Bell's office. Mike feels good about himself. He and his Dad go straight to the swimming pool.

3

Habits
and
Hypnosis

Sue bites her fingernails. She bites them so short that her fingers hurt. Furthermore, she hates the way her hands look. She says to herself. "I'm going to try harder than I've ever tried before to quit biting my fingernails."

Sounds good, doesn't it? But it doesn't work so well. In the 1920s a man named Emile Coué studied this kind of will-power. Among many other things he learned that "I'll try"

Emile Coué.

usually means "I'll try but I don't think I can." Coué called this fact the "Law of Reversed Effect." Sue *really* believes that she *can't* quit biting her nails, and the harder she tries to quit, the more she bites. Sometimes willpower works, and bad habits disappear—at least for a while. More often, willpower leads to failure. The reason is that, deep down, failure is expected.

Sue tried hard. She used all the willpower she could muster to quit biting her fingernails. She put tape over them, she painted them with terrible-tasting stuff. But she even bit her nails in her sleep. Finally, she and her parents went to a hypnotherapist.

Sue's hypnotherapist, Dr. Mann, is a psychologist. Dr. Mann explains that when she bit her nails for the first time, it probably comforted her. Whenever she needs comforting, whenever she feels the way she felt that first time, she will bite her nails. Her subconscious believes that biting her nails can still comfort her. Hypnosis will take her back to that first time.

Dr. Mann leads Sue into hypnosis. As he gives Sue the right suggestions, she seems to travel back in time. She forgets, for the moment, that she's eleven. She watches what she did at younger ages, feels what she felt then, tastes things she tasted then. Finally, as Dr. Mann suggests, she arrives back at the very first time she bit her fingernails. She was very little, and she was hungry. Because she was hungry, her stomach hurt, and because her stomach hurt she was scared. She put her fingers into her mouth and chewed on them. That made her feel better.

Dr. Mann knows that Sue was only hungry for a little while. He also knows that it seemed like a long time to her. He decides to give her a new memory of the event. He suggests to her subconscious that her mother came quickly, picked her up, hugged her and fed her—which is probably exactly what really happened. He suggests that Sue really didn't have time to chew her fingernails. He also suggests that she wasn't really scared.

Sue's subconscious still knows that she was scared. It also knows that she really bit her fingernails and that it made her feel better at the time. Dr. Mann has simply convinced her subconscious to pretend that something else happened instead. Since her subconscious is willing to pretend that she never bit her nails, and therefore wasn't comforted by it, Sue has no remembered need to bite her nails when she's nervous or hungry.

Dr. Mann brings Sue back to the present, although she is still hypnotized. He gives her suggestions about how nice her life will be with longer fingernails. With the help of the doctor's suggestions, Sue sees long fingernails on her hands. She sees their nice shape and feels how comfortable her fingers feel. She hears people complimenting her hands, and she feels proud.

Dr. Mann believes that the subconscious mind is a memory bank, and that memories can be summoned up from the subconscious and changed. Other qualified hypnotherapists might have used other methods to change Sue's habit. They might suggest that from then on Sue would have more self-control. When her hands started toward her mouth, she would be aware of them and put them elsewhere. The therapist would probably add that she'd see some progress right away, and that it would increase. Still other hypnotherapists might suggest a different brand of willpower—the brand that says, "I will," instead of "I'll try."

There are as many ways to lead a person into hypnosis, and to use it, as there are hypnotherapists. Each hypnotherapist has a method that works well for him or her. But one thing every hypnotherapist knows is how to give good suggestions.

Coué taught that positive suggestions are stronger than negative ones. He also taught that the subconscious is stronger than the conscious. Whenever the two disagree, the subconscious will always win the argument. In Sue's case, her subconscious need to keep on biting her nails was stronger than her conscious wish to stop. She ended her habit only after her subconscious agreed that she no longer needed it. That's why we need a way to get in touch with our subconscious minds. Hypnosis is one of the best ways we know.

There are many bad habits that hypnotherapists can help solve. They can also solve more serious problems. We've already seen that Mike overcame his great fear of water with hypnosis. Such a fear is called a *phobia*. There are numerous phobias—of heights, closed-in places, flying, the water, and many others—and hypnotherapists can help with all of them. They also help with problems such as smoking, overeating, stuttering, blushing, acne, bed-wetting, alcoholism, and drug abuse.

Just as hypnosis can help overcome bad habits, it can help create good habits. Athletes sometimes use hypnosis to help them perform better. Jack is a hurdler, but lately he can't get his back leg cleanly over the hurdles. He exercises that leg, he practices by the hour, but the leg still knocks down hurdles. He's disgusted with himself. Then he visits a hypnotherapist who, with the right suggestions, helps Jack solve his problem.

Of course, hypnosis can't turn a person with no athletic ability into a super athlete. Neither can it turn just anyone into an opera star. But hypnosis can help to improve the talents and skills that we already have.

Hypnosis helps actors remember their lines and step into character when the cameras roll. Students use hypnosis to help them remember what they study. Some people suffer stage fright when they have to make a speech or perform in front of people. With the help of hypnosis, they can learn to relax before an audience.

A skilled, qualified hypnotherapist can help with these and many other problems. But the words "skilled" and "qualified" are very important. What if a friend told you he could fix your cavity? Would you let him? Of course not. He sure doesn't know as much about teeth as your dentist!

Just learning how to lead someone into hypnosis is not difficult. There are many books that explain how. But the books can't give experience—knowing what to say. We've seen how very important suggestions are in hypnosis. Hypnotherapists are word experts. They know how to make good suggestions. Someone who didn't know what he or she was doing would be likely to give poor suggestions.

What makes a hypnotherapist qualified? Where do hypnotherapists get experience? Many have gone to special schools where they practiced under experts until they, too, became expert and certified as hypnotherapists. A qualified hypnotherapist may also be a psychologist, a psychiatrist, a medical doctor, or a dentist. Qualified hypnotherapists will always discuss their qualifications on request.

4

More Uses of Hypnosis

Maxine stutters so much that few people take the time to listen to her. Maxine's parents hear that hypnosis might help her. They visit several hypnotherapists to find one they like. They finally reach Mike Howe, a certified hypnotherapist who specializes in helping young people. They hope Mr. Howe can help Maxine.

Maxine's hands quiver as she shakes Mr. Howe's hand. He

leads her and her mother into his office and asks them to sit down. Maxine glances around. Mr. Howe's office looks more like a living room than an office. It is a quiet, comfortable room.

Mr. Howe asks Maxine questions about herself. What grade is she in? Does she like school? What are her hobbies? Her nervousness makes Maxine stutter more than ever. Mr. Howe listens patiently while she struggles with the words. Slowly Maxine relaxes, and the words come easier. Mr. Howe makes her feel confident that hypnosis will cure her stuttering.

Mr. Howe asks if Maxine is ready to start and she nods. She lies down comfortably on the sofa. Mr. Howe tells her to take deep breaths, to hold them, then to let all the air out slowly. He compliments her on how well she relaxes and says that in a moment she will find that her mind is relaxed, too.

Mr. Howe says, "All right, Maxine, on the count of three, try to think of your telephone number. You'll be surprised to discover that it's gone. Later, when you're out of hypnosis, the number will be right where it always was, but, for now, the numbers are missing. As you search for them, you'll go deeper into hypnosis. Ready? One . . . two . . . three."

Maxine tries hard. She finds the first number and says, "Five." Then the other numbers slide away.

"Can you find the other numbers?" Mr. Howe asks.

"No," Maxine says in amazement.

Mr. Howe proceeds to give Maxine suggestions that when she speaks she will say the words easily. She'll feel relaxed and will be able to speak as clearly as everyone else. He asks Maxine to see herself standing on the stage in the school auditorium and tells her to give a speech about George Washington.

Maxine hears herself declare, "George Washington was the first president of the United States." She is amazed. She isn't stuttering.

Mr. Howe exclaims, "Very good, Maxine! Listen to all the clapping. Look how everyone is smiling and nodding. Everyone is impressed with how well you spoke. You're proud and sure of yourself, and you should be. Everyone is proud of you!"

He finishes by giving Maxine instructions on how to put herself into hypnosis to help herself if she stutters. He says that she will leave hypnosis feeling wonderful and knowing that from that day on she will always speak clearly.

As Mr. Howe leads her out of hypnosis, Maxine smiles and says, "Thanks, Mr. Howe. It really felt good to be giving a speech . . ." She remembers what happened under hypnosis. But then she stops and spins toward her mother. "Mom! Listen to me!" she exclaims "I'm not stuttering. Isn't it great!"

Some dentists use hypnosis as anesthesia. Many people are terrified of having dental work done. Dr. Ames knows this, and she wants her patients to feel comfortable and relaxed while she works. She wants them to enjoy coming to her office.

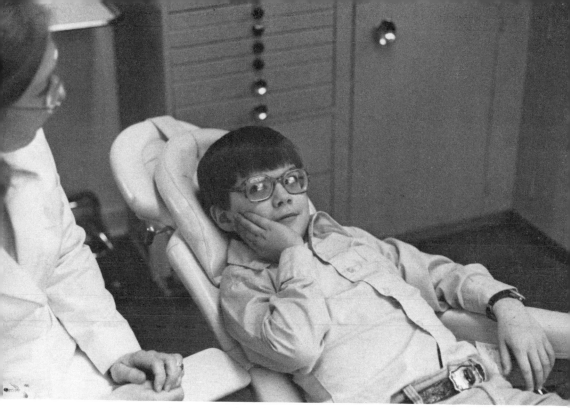

Wow! No shot and it's numb!

Dr. Ames learned about hypnosis in dental school and took extra classes that taught her how to use it. She can quickly hypnotize just about anyone. But Carl's feet drag as he follows Dr. Ames into her office. Dr. Ames explains that Carl will have fun while he's there. Carl thinks she's crazy, but he decides to go along. Dr. Ames explains that while she fixes his tooth he can feel anything he chooses to feel. He can feel a sparkle, a tickle, or he can feel numb. Carl chooses numb, and

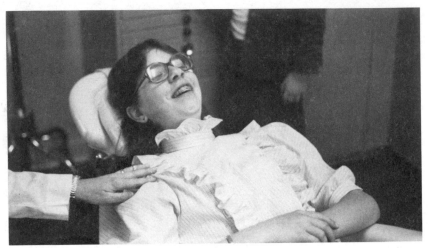

Whenever you need to go deeper into hypnosis, a touch
on the shoulder or wrist will do it.

Dr. Ames quickly leads him into hypnosis. Carl is amazed to
find that hypnosis numbs his mouth better than the shots he
hates. Dr. Ames tells Carl that the work will take only a few
minutes and that while she works he can watch his favorite
movie. "Okay, Carl, the movie is starting. Is the sound loud
enough?" Carl nods and concentrates on watching the movie.
He knows he is really in a dentist's chair, and he knows there
is really no movie. But he watches it as he sits there just as
surely as he'd watch it in the movie theater.

When the movie ends, Carl's tooth is fixed. He'd only been there 15 minutes, yet he'd seen the whole movie. He hadn't been scared or hurt while Dr. Ames fixed his tooth and the numbness disappeared as soon as Dr. Ames led him out of hypnosis. His mouth feels normal and good.

A medical doctor might use hypnosis to numb a patients's arm before giving a shot or stitching a cut. But in medicine hypnosis has other uses as well.

Many sicknesses are called *psychosomatic* (sy-koh-so-MAT-ik). *Psycho* refers to mind, *somatic* to body. A psychosomatic illness is one that is caused by the mind. Some people think psychosomatic illnesses are fake. They're wrong. Psychosomatic illnesses are very real indeed.

It's a good movie.

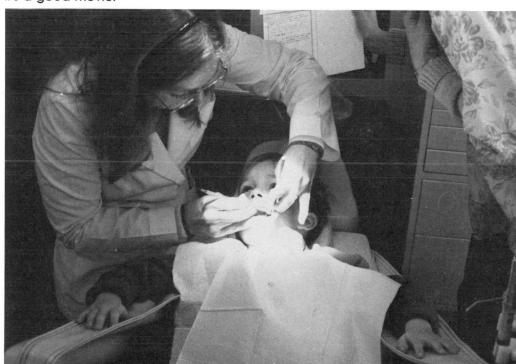

Most common headaches are psychosomatic. And if you've ever had one, you know a headache is real. It hurts! Self-hypnosis can get rid of some common headaches. It works much faster than aspirin or anything else.

Some experts even believe that *all* sicknesses are psychosomatic and can be cured with mind power. Maybe they're right, or maybe they're wrong. Science doesn't know for sure as yet.

There is some proof that many allergies are psychosomatic. There are many other health problems with psychosomatic factors. Among them are asthma, backaches, migraine headaches, skin problems, arthritis, flu, insomnia, the common cold, ulcers, and high blood pressure. Hypnosis can help to cure them all.

How can illness come from the subconscious mind which is supposed to protect us? The subconscious mind is very complicated. Sometimes it protects us from one thing by letting another thing hurt us.

Take Sandra's allergy to daisies. No other flowers made her sneeze and itch, but the moment she got near a daisy she sneezed and itched and was so miserable she had to leave. One day she started sneezing and scratching in a store. Her father looked around and spotted a huge bouquet of daisies. He walked over to them and was shocked to discover that they were made of cloth. He called Sandra over. As soon as she discovered the daisies were fake, she stopped sneezing and itching. She felt silly and confused. How could daisies made of cloth cause her to sneeze?

Sandra and her father visited a hypnotherapist who took her back to the first time she saw a daisy. She was a toddler. She reached out and pulled the flower closer. Unfortunately, there was a bee on the daisy, and it stung her. That was when Sandra's subconscious mind decided to protect her from bee stings in the future by keeping her away from daisies.

In hypnosis, Sandra learned that she no longer needed to itch and sneeze when she saw a daisy. Now she can enjoy the daisies that she always thought were so pretty.

Some doctors use a combination of hypnosis and regular medicines and treatments. These doctors encourage their patients' minds to work harder to combat illness. They also know when it is necessary to help with medications and surgery. They balance mind and medical power. Sometimes medical doctors who haven't themselves studied hypnosis work with hypnotherapists to combine medical and mind power. Still other doctors, for many reasons, choose not to use hypnosis at all. If their patients wish to combine medicine with hypnosis, however, they may recommend certified hypnotherapists.

The fact that hypnosis helps people cure themselves of many problems is proven. We have yet to learn whether or not hypnosis can help cure more illnesses. And we have also to find out exactly which illnesses are truly psychosomatic.

Sometimes psychosomatic illnesses are caused by sugges-

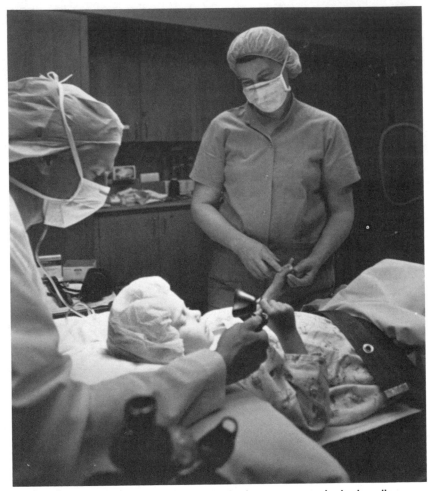

Teamed with medical treatment, mind power can help healing.

tions that are called "organ language." These may be either self-suggestions or suggestions from other people. A person who constantly says, "That gives me a pain in the neck," may sooner or later get a very real pain in the neck.

A person who uses lots of salt on his food might be constantly told, "If you keep eating so much salt, you'll get high blood pressure." Of course, this suggestion is meant to convince him to use less salt. But if he chooses to continue eating huge amounts of it, what will happen? His blood pressure will go up. Is the salt to blame or is the suggestion to blame? Some experts believe it's the salt, but others think the very suggestion of high blood pressure can be responsible for raising it. From what we know of the power of suggestion, it seems probable that the suggestion is at least partially responsible.

In hypnosis, suggestions are repeated many times. They are positive suggestions, good and helpful ones. Eventually the suggestions help us overcome problems. Suggestions to combat illness can work in the same way. Awareness of how suggestions affect us helps us to be able to reject those for illness and accept only suggestions for being well. Hypnotherapists can help by teaching their patients how to use self-hypnosis to fend off suggestions for illness.

Most experts agree that self-hypnosis is perfectly safe. It's also interesting and fun. "But," you might exclaim, "I don't know enough about minds and suggestions. You just said so!"

You know one mind well enough. Your own. Your mind knows itself. Your subconscious will not let you harm it—or yourself—with your own suggestions. One of the most important jobs your subconscious has is to protect you. The subconscious will reject poor suggestions.

Many hypnotherapists may give their patients tape-recorded suggestions that they can use at home. In this type of self-hypnosis, it isn't necessary to create your own suggestions. An expert has done it for you. Self-hypnosis tapes are also available in stores and through mail-order houses but should be used only when recommended by a therapist.

With self-hypnosis, we can reinforce suggestions given to us in hypnotherapy sessions, we can cure ourselves of hiccoughs and most headaches, give ourselves suggestions for good study habits, for improving our talents, ending bad habits, and for many other things as well.

Now let's take a look at the lighter side of hypnosis.

5

The Stage Hypnotist

Stage hypnosis is related to, but different from, scientific hypnosis. Purpose is the biggest difference. The sole purpose of stage hypnosis is fun.

The stage hypnotist is a performing artist—like a comic or a singer. If anything, the stage hypnotist relies even more on the audience than do other stage performers. The stage hypnotist's act is to guide audience volunteers through hypnotic

Ormond McGill, famed stage hypnotist, says that a stageful of hypnotized subjects and lots of action make exciting entertainment.

stunts. These stunts provide the laughs and gasps that make the show.

Many people believe that stage hypnotism is phony, that the volunteers aren't hypnotized and that most are plants—people paid by the hypnotist to pretend to be hypnotized. That can sometimes happen.

Anyone who's read *The Adventures of Tom Sawyer* by Mark Twain, can easily imagine that Mark Twain, himself, was quite a character. His real name was Samuel Clemens. When he was young, Samuel went with a friend to a hypnosis show that came to town. The hypnotist asked for volunteers, and the two boys dashed onto the stage. Sam's friend was quickly

Ormond McGill was a pioneer in presenting demonstrations of hypnotism on TV — here with Art Linkletter and a group of hypnotized subjects on the ABC "People Are Funny" show.

Samuel Clemens, known as Mark Twain, performed with a stage hypnotist when he was a boy.

hypnotized and went into a deep trance. Sam didn't. Nevertheless, he got into the spirit of the show and followed all the instructions with great flair. The audience loved him. So did the hypnotist. And for the rest of the shows in that town, Samuel Clemens was a plant who performed with the real volunteers.

Undoubtedly, inexperienced or incompetent stage hypnotists still rely on similar tricks. Successful stage hypnotists, however, really do hypnotize their volunteers, and, if they do use plants, the plants are also hypnotized.

Let's sit in on one of Madam Felicia's shows. Her real name is Babs Smith. She likes her real name but, face it, Babs Smith has less pizazz than Madam Felicia, and a stage hypnotist needs a catchy name.

Madam Felicia is a show person. She wears an elaborate, slightly mysterious costume. She makes passes with her hands in much the same way that Mesmer did in the 1700s. She uses stage props. Sometimes she even uses a wand. Colored lights create a mysterious and expectant mood.

Madam Felicia begins her show by talking about hypnosis. She explains it differently from the way a hypnotherapist would. She explains hypnosis as a fun, slightly strange experience. But she does cover the basic facts. This done, Madam Felicia asks if ten people will come on stage to be hypnotized.

Ben grins as he hurries onto the stage. He's a fun-loving guy and if, as he expects, he ends up doing some goofy things, that's okay with him. Madam Felicia begins with a demonstration of *waking hypnosis*. This is simple suggestion. She suggests to a girl that she's falling backward. Soon the girl is convinced she is falling—and Madam Felicia has to catch her as soon as she begins to fall. She convinces two people that their right arms have turned to steel and will not bend. Then she convinces Ben that a stick is glued to his hands.

Ben is amazed and slightly scared when he finds that he really can't let go of the stick. Madam Felicia watches as he struggles, then announces that the glue has dissolved and he can now drop the stick. Ben's mouth falls open as the stick drops from his hands. The audience howls with glee. Ben feels like a puppet. He begins to wonder about himself and about Madam Felicia. If she can make him do such things without even hypnotizing him, what might she make him do under hypnosis? Maybe she lied about hypnosis. Maybe she lied when she said she wouldn't make the volunteers do things she, herself, wouldn't do. Maybe she'd do things Ben wouldn't do. What if she really had strange powers and forced Ben to take off his pants or do something equally outrageous?

Meanwhile, two people don't follow Madam Felicia's suggestions. They won't be easy to hypnotize, so she sends them back into the audience. She keeps Ben and the others on stage, because they are the most likely to help her put on a good show.

Ben's glad he wasn't sent off the stage. He'd be mortified if that happened to him. But now he's nervous about what is to come. He notices for the first time that the audience is huge. What will all those people think of him after the show? As Madam Felicia begins to hypnotize, Ben's concentration is divided between her and the people in the audience. Sure enough, he doesn't enter hypnosis.

His face flames as Madam Felicia quietly tells him that he should return to his seat. He barely hears her thank him, and he ignores her assurances that another time, if he wants to, he'll be able to enter hypnosis. In fact, as he shuffles back to his seat, avoiding the eyes that turn his way, he decides he must be too smart to be hypnotized. He's too smart to let the likes of Madam Felicia make a fool of him.

Back on stage, Madam Felicia has begun to put her seven remaining subjects through some hypnotic paces. She hands Beth a glass of water and tells her it's sour lemon juice but that she must drink it. The audience roars as Beth's lips and face pucker up as she struggles to swallow the water.

Madam Felicia convinces Ralph that he's stuck to his chair. He tries and tries, but he can't get away from his chair.

Madam Felicia then convinces all seven people on the stage that they're a famous rock group, and commands them to perform. The audience loves the horrendous screeching—and so do the "rock stars."

Madam Felicia stops the rock performance and tells the volunteers to sit down again. She places them even deeper into hypnosis, then tells them she will awaken them and send them back to their seats but that five minutes later they will stand up and say the Pledge of Allegiance to the Flag. Madam

Ormond McGill hypnotizes a subject into believing he has X-ray vision — more fun than embarrassing.

Profound hypnosis in a subject.

Felicia then awakens them, thanks them, and, amidst thunderous clapping, the seven return to their seats.

Madam Felicia goes on with her show. Suddenly, just five minutes after she has dismissed them, the seven volunteers get an irresistable urge to stand up and recite the Pledge of Allegiance. Feeling foolish, they still do as they were told to while under hypnosis.

Madam Felicia hypnotizes people in a much different way from a therapist. Her goal is different, it's entertainment for audience approval. Many therapeutic hypnotherapists, however, think stage hypnotism should be against the law. (It is illegal in England.) They say it's dangerous to let untrained people probe minds. They might point to Ben and say he was damaged by his experience because of his embarrassment.

But Madam Felicia *is* a skilled hypnotist. She is not a therapist, and she knows it. She has no interest in probing people's minds. Her audience wouldn't enjoy such a serious demonstration of hypnosis, nor would she risk hurting her volunteers in any way. She simply demonstrates the powers of the mind. Madam Felicia is as skilled in giving her variety of suggestions as hypnotherapists are in giving theirs. And she's learned how to spot the people who are not suggestible or who might need to be quickly led away from hypnosis.

Still, hypnotherapists worry that the feeling and image of magic that the stage hypnotist encourages might discourage the serious usage of hypnotism for curing.

The Detective, the Lawyer, and the Judge

After the fear and excitement of a crime or accident, details about what happened often blur. Different people remember the details differently.

Say, for instance, that you're walking along a lonely street very early in the morning. You notice two men walking toward you but you pay scant attention to them. Suddenly, one man shoves the other into an alley and starts beating him up.

You see it happen, but you certainly don't stick around. For one thing, the mugger is so much bigger than you that you couldn't stop him even if you tried. Besides, you must hurry and call the police. Just as you dash away, you see the mugger reach into the victim's pockets.

By the time the police arrive, the mugger has fled and his victim is moaning. The police ask you what the mugger looked like. You try to describe him. The police exchange defeated glances. From your description, the mugger could be anyone.

However, the police ask if you'd be willing to go into hypnosis. They explain that you could probably give a more complete description of the mugger that way. You agree. (In some states parents must also give permission for people under 18 to be hypnotized.)

Under hypnosis, you go back to just before the crime occurred. You're again walking along the street. The hypnotist asks you to describe every detail of your walk. You hear yourself describing the cars parked along the curb—the same cars you barely noticed earlier. You describe the buildings you are passing. You even recall the long crack that ran along the middle of the sidewalk for half a block. Then you see two men walking toward you, the victim and the mugger. Under hypnosis, you see that the mugger's hair is reddish-brown, parted on the left, and scraggly—as if it hasn't been combed for a long time. His eyes are close together and he has crooked, yellow teeth. He walks with an uneven step. You compare his height and weight to the victims's much more accurately than before.

When you've described every detail recorded in your sub-conscious mind, the therapist leads you out of hypnosis. The police artist hands you a sketch made from your description. Your eyes pop wide open and you exclaim, "That's him!"

Under hypnosis, witnesses remember license plate numbers and other exact details about accidents or crimes. There are some experts, however, who question the reliability of hypnotic recall. Not all experts believe that the subconscious functions like an instant replay TV set. They feel it is possible for a subject under hypnosis to confuse images in the brain. He or she may mix up a scene remembered from a movie with a real crime scene, for instance. This is called *misplaced recall*. Some experts believe that people can even lie in hyp-nosis. After all, they argue, the hypnotherapist has no power, so the hypnotized subject can lie if he or she wants to. Other experts believe that people always tell the truth in hypnosis. The skilled hypnotherapist carefully constructs suggestions to encourage truthful recall and discourage misplaced recall, but it's still impossible to know for sure if a hypnotized person is describing what really happened or what he or she thinks may have happened. Sometimes lie detectors are used to help judge the truth, but lie detectors work only if the subject believes he or she is lying. Lie detectors are of no use if the hypnotized person believes he or she is telling the truth.

Let's consider the person who claims that an evil hypnotist convinced him or her to commit a crime against his or her will. Experts are sharply divided as to whether or not this is possible. Experts who believe this is possible say that it can be done by altering a person's view of reality—for instance, by convincing a subject that in order to prevent the overthrow of the government he must kill a certain person or steal a certain item. These experts point to laboratory tests where, in controlled situations, people have been convinced to behave in an antisocial manner. They also point to actual crimes that are said to have been committed because of the use of hypnosis. Other experts, however, insist that it is impossible to make a hypnotized subject commit a crime. Not a single case in which a crime was supposedly committed under hypnosis has ever been adequately documented. In every case, the "unwilling" perpetrator has already had a criminal record or shown criminal tendencies. In the case of laboratory experiments, the subjects know they are in a controlled situation and that their actions are unlikely to cause real harm. Critics therefore, insist that these laboratory tests have no relationship to actual life situations.

As we learn more about hypnosis, we will know better whether it is a useful tool in the search for justice.

ESP

ESP—*extrasensory perception*—is often called the "sixth sense." It is everything we somehow know but can't see, hear, smell, taste or touch.

ESP is a catchall term for several different mental skills. One of these skills is *telepathy*, another word for mind reading. Telepathy is what most people think of when they hear the term ESP. As with other forms of ESP, telepathy is studied both in everyday living and in the laboratory by parapsychologists.

Everyday telepathy is mystifying and interesting but is almost impossible to prove. Let's say Brenda is watching TV when the phone rings. Even before she answers it, she "knows" that Ann is calling. To her delight she is correct. The girls wonder if it's telepathy.

If they were both watching the same TV show, telepathy was probably not involved. More likely, something in the show made each girl think of the other. It might have been the way an actor moved, a bit of dialogue, or the scenery. Consciously, the girls don't know what it was, but their subconscious minds each saw the same cue. That cue made each girl think about the other.

If, however, Brenda was watching TV and Ann was reading just before the phone call, the probability of telepathy in action is better. But it is still hard to prove.

Telepathy experiments in laboratories use strict conditions that remove all *sensory* cues—all cues that can be seen, heard, smelled, touched or tasted. Many telepathy experiments use ESP Cards, sometimes called Zener Cards for Karl Zener who helped design them.

An ESP deck has twenty-five cards in all. There are five cards with circles on them, five with squares, five with stars, five with crosses and five with wavy lines.

Two people take part in a telepathy experiment, a "sender" and a "receiver." The sender shuffles the deck, then turns over each card, one at a time, concentrating on the name of the design he or she sees. The sender tries to send this thought

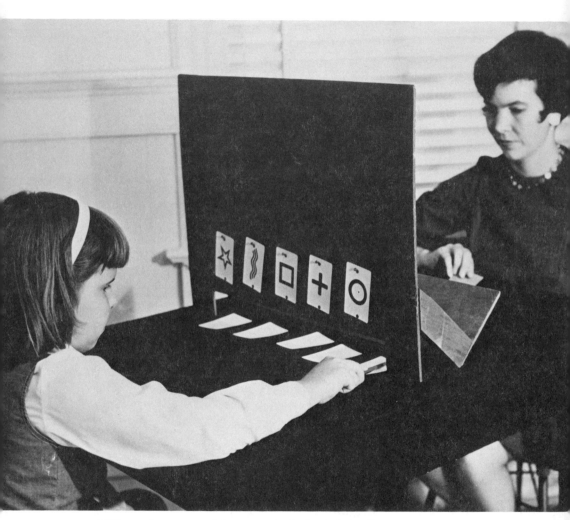

ESP cards are used in some tests for telepathy.

message about the design to the receiver. The receiver keeps his or her mind blank and open so he or she can receive the message. When he or she receives a thought, it is told to the experimenter, who checks to see if it is correct.

Parapsychologists have figured out how many cards can be named correctly simply by guesswork or chance. More than this number shows real telepathy. For instance, on a true/false history test with one hundred questions, let's say you could get 50 right if you knew no history at all. Such a score would make your teacher wonder if you'd even opened your history book before the test. If, however, you got 90 questions right, she would know that you'd studied. The odds say that you couldn't get 90 questions right just by guesswork.

Just as with the true/false test, if the telepathic receiver names enough cards correctly, we can be sure that it's the result of telepathy rather than lucky guesses. The receivers and senders never know if they've been successful until they are told by the experimenter. Even people who score amazingly high don't know—any more than Brenda knew for sure that Ann was calling until she heard Ann's voice. How telepathy happens is still very much a mystery.

Many experts believe that we all have telepathic abilities but that they've rusted, so to speak, from disuse. Some believe that babies are born telepathic. They believe that babies and their mothers "talk" with telepathy until the baby is old enough to vocalize its wants and needs. Then, according to this theory, the baby begins to build mental barriers against its mother's thoughts. As the child grows, the barriers get stronger until all telepathic communication is blocked. But those whose minds did not build barriers grow into adult telepaths.

Telepathic messages are more likely to be received if they are "shouted." When the sender is very happy, or terrified, or furious, the message is stronger than if the sender is calm. While some people seem able to receive calm thoughts, more people are able to receive "shouted" thoughts. But most people are either unwilling or unable to receive the loudest thoughts, the mental scream.

Clairvoyance is an ESP skill that is very similar to telepathy. In telepathy, a thought pops into the receiver's mind. In clairvoyance, a picture pops into the receiver's mind. Clairvoyance means "clear seeing." Since telepathy and clairvoyance are so much alike, many experts lump the two together and call them *General ESP*.

One afternoon, Seth sat in his room listening to records. Suddenly he "saw" a bird's-eye view of a place thirty miles away. He couldn't understand it. Later, his best friend called to say that he'd gone hang gliding at that place that afternoon. He had looked down and wished that Seth could have been there with him. Is this a clairvoyant experience? If Seth didn't know that his friend would be gliding that day, it might be. But this kind of experience is hard to prove as clairvoyance. It might be coincidence, or two people with similar interests zooming in on the same subject and later thinking it was at the same time. Parapsychologists try to prove clairvoyance in the laboratory instead.

In many clairvoyance tests pictures are sealed inside envelopes that are impossible to see through. A person being tested must either sketch or describe the picture inside without opening the envelope. In this way, it has been proven that some people are skilled clairvoyants.

Another ESP skill is *precognition*. Precognition means knowing something will happen before it does. Sometimes it has to do with something good, at other times, it's something bad. Maybe you've heard of someone who says, after a plane crash, "Just think, I should have been on that flight but I had a feeling it would crash so I took another flight!" This appears to be precognition, but is it? There's no way to prove it one way or the other. Maybe whenever that person stepped into a plane he or she "knew" it would crash, but it never did.

People receive precognition thoughts in many ways, but the most common seems to be in dreams. When they are dreaming they "see" something that hasn't happened. Sometimes they remember the dreams vividly. Other times they're forgotten until the event actually happens. Some people believe that feelings of *déjà vu*, of something seen or felt before, are the result of precognition. Déjà vu is the spooky feeling you get when you're at some place you've never been to before, yet suddenly everything is familiar. Perhaps it's the result of a

In this precognition test, the subject predicts which light will come on next and pushes the button beneath that light to indicate her choice. Lights come on one at a time, in a different order each time.

precognitive dream that you've forgotten. Perhaps there is something about this place that's similar to another place you've visited. As with other types of ESP, precognition is difficult to prove.

There is, however, one very visible type of ESP. It's called *psychokinesis*. This is the act of moving or changing an object with mind power alone. As in other forms of ESP, those who have the gift of psychokinesis don't know how it happens. A very puzzling problem for people with psychokinetic abilities is that sometimes they can't control them. They cannot always call on them or stop them when they want.

Imagine how scared you'd be if suddenly a chair leaped to the ceiling, hovered there a few moments, then crashed back to the floor. It would be tempting to believe in *poltergeists* or mischievious ghosts. However, many parapsychologists believe that a poltergeist is really a troubled teenager with psychokinetic abilities. They've found that psychokinetic activity usually ends when the teen is removed from the premises or finds other ways to cope with the problems of maturing.

In laboratory experiments for psychokinetic ability, people bend "unbendable" materials with mind power alone. These experiments are so carefully controlled that there is no possibility of cheating.

Psychokinetic parties can be fun. At these parties, young people learn to bend metal objects simply through the use of individual and group concentration. Out of more than 1,000 people tested by one experimenter, 85% were able to "warm bend" metal objects such as silverware and metal rods. The term "warm bending" refers to the heat released by an object as it bends.

These, then, are the various forms of extrasensory perception. For many years people have been trying to prove whether or not they really exist. The best evidence indicates that they do—at least on a limited basis. But what does ESP have to do with hypnosis? Both ESP and hypnosis require concentration. The trancelike appearance of some people in hypnosis and people doing some ESP tests is similar. Young people seem to be better subjects for both. Creative people are better at both than less creative people. Finally, people who believe they can enter hypnosis, enter it more easily than people who believe they can't. Likewise, people who believe in ESP and believe they have some talent for it are more likely to experience ESP than people who believe it's a hoax.

But the connections go beyond these similarities. One of the main connections between hypnosis and ESP is their common history. It was Franz Anton Mesmer's studies that first interested scientists in the unusual powers of the mind. ESP experiences are quite common in hypnosis sessions. The history of hypnosis is full of them. In the 1700s, for instance, a hypnotized woman described a burning laboratory located many miles away. Later, it was learned that the laboratory she described really was burning at the precise moment she "saw" the fire.

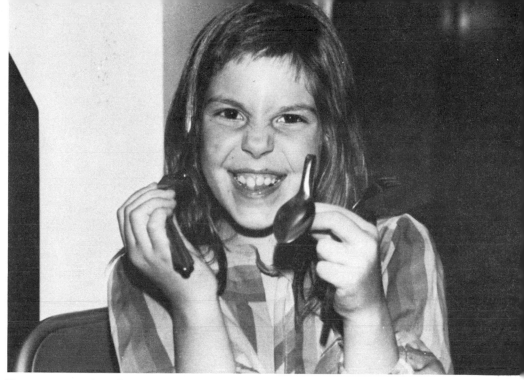

These youngsters have just bent the utensils they are holding by mind power alone.

It seems that we let down some of our mental barriers when we enter hypnosis. This doesn't mean that a hypnotist can read our minds. Quite the contrary. The hypnotized person seems more likely to receive the hypnotist's thoughts or have other extrasensory perceptions.

Hypnosis enhances ESP experiences for many people. For that reason, hypnosis is sometimes used to help develop natural ESP talents in much the same way that athletes use hypnosis to improve athletic abilities.

8

Reincarnation

Reincarnation means living time and time again. The theory of reincarnation is so close to religion that it is a very explosive topic. However, reincarnation has also been so closely linked to hypnosis that no discussion of hypnosis can be complete without a few words about it.

The basic idea of reincarnation is that the human soul lives forever in different forms and in different bodies. Beyond this, people's ideas on the subject split in different directions. Some say that the soul is reborn into a new body the moment the old body dies. Others say that souls may live in two different bodies at the same time. Some say that souls live in a spirit world between lives. Still others say we've all lived lives as various plants, animals, and people. Most theories seem to agree that a soul comes closer to perfection with each new life. A person's human lives might include a life as a slave in ancient Egypt helping to build a pyramid, a lady-in-waiting at the court of Queen Elizabeth I, and an American Indian during the settlement of the American West.

People who believe in reincarnation believe that it explains many mysteries. It explains, they say, how people become geniuses. It explains that déjà vu is a flashback to an experience in a previous life, and some believe that reincarnation explains ghosts. Ghosts, they say, are spirits who have not yet gone on to a new life.

In some of the world's religions reincarnation is accepted as fact. Christians who believe in reincarnation say the Bible talks of reincarnation. Other Christians believe the Bible denies reincarnation.

Some hypnotists search for proof about reincarnation. We've seen how, in hypnosis, some people seem able to turn back the clock to earlier years in their lifetimes. Some experts believe that the subconscious has recorded previous lifetimes as well as the person's current life. Thousands of people are said to have been hypnotically regressed to past lives. They relive these lives with as much detail as you'd expect to hear from friends describing their recent vacations. They give names and descriptions of places and people just as though they were there again. They can often recall or relive their births and their deaths and tell how these events affected them and the people around them.

Many describe a spirit world in which they stayed between lives. These descriptions vary from one person to another, but most describe a bright light and a feeling of warmth, and all are amazingly alike. The spirit world they describe is a contented place. They have no bodies, they can be with anyone they choose, they are never hungry or angry or sad. They all eventually have to live again, something which they do not look forward to doing. Some describe a universal consciousness that knows everything. None, however, believe they've been with God; most feel that they weren't yet ready to be with God.

Do these experiences prove the theory of reincarnation? Perhaps they do for those who have lived them. For the rest of us, however, the experiences are, at best, only circumstantial evidence in support of the theories of reincarnation. Hard, indisputable, scientific proof is still lacking in this mystery, as it is with other mysteries of the mind.

Perhaps someday scientists will unlock all these mysteries. Then we'll know if reincarnation, ESP, and hypnotic experiences are real. Until that day, we can each study and learn and form our own opinions based on the available evidence. There is an ever-growing library of information you can consult.

Some Fun
with
Hypnosis

Stage hypnotists often include animal hypnosis in their shows. Animal hypnosis is really not hypnosis at all. It is called hypnosis because it looks a little like human hypnosis. It's the trick of putting animals in a certain position so that they remain that way, almost as if asleep, until moved. You certainly couldn't make a chicken bark or a lobster meow.

You probably couldn't hypnotize your family pet because it's used to being handled. Animals that aren't pets and that don't know you are much easier to hypnotize. Of course, you're gentle in your handling of these animals. With a little practice and patience you can learn to hypnotize a variety of animals.

Chickens are probably the easiest of all animals to "hypnotize." Gently, but firmly, grasp the chicken and put its beak to the floor or the ground. Hold it there for a few seconds and draw a line straight out in front of the chicken's beak for about two feet. The chicken may struggle until the line is drawn or it may struggle only until its beak touches the ground. If it continues to struggle after the line is drawn, don't worry about it. It will calm down quickly and become very still. It is "hypnotized." If left alone, it would stay put for up to two hours. To awaken it sooner, simply nudge its beak away from the

Holding the chickens' beaks to the ground and drawing a line out from each beak, immobilizes the chickens.

The chickens will stay like this for up to two hours before they slowly rise and run off squawking.

line. It will seem confused for a moment, then will probably run off squawking and flapping its wings.

To "hypnotize" a rabbit, gently but firmly pick it up and lay it on its back. With one hand, gently separate the ears and lay them against the ground or a tabletop. Using your other hand, stretch out the hind legs and hold them against the table. Wait thirty seconds or so until you feel the rabbit relaxing, then slowly remove your hands. The rabbit will stay put. To awaken the rabbit, simply roll it onto its side. It will immediately get to its feet and begin to hop around. The rabbit would also eventually awaken on its own.

Guinea pigs are "hypnotized" much like rabbits. Awaken them by standing them on their feet.

Place a rabbit on its back, lay the ears against the table, and hold the hind legs.

When the rabbit has relaxed, slowly remove your hands.

Frogs can be "hypnotized" by laying them on their backs. Nudge them with you finger to awaken them and they'll usually roll onto their feet. If they don't, you can put them back on their feet.

Lobsters can be "hypnotized" by standing them on their heads and balancing them with their claws. They, too, wake up when they're replaced in a normal position.

Have you ever heard of fish stroking? Catch a fish in a net, of course keeping it under water, and gently stroke its side for a few seconds. The fish will go limp in the water.

With a little practice you can become good at "hypnotizing" these and other animals. Don't worry about having to find

Even a frog can be "hypnotized."

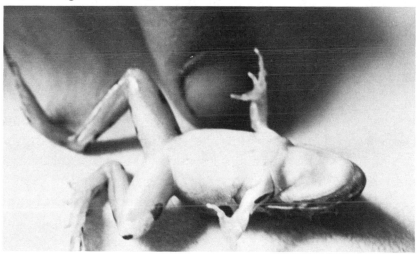

new animals each time. The same animals will come to expect you to "hypnotize" them and, as long as you treat them kindly, they'll continue to perform for you. To add excitement, you might make up a speech to recite as you position the animals. Stage hypnotists use speeches, called patters, for dramatic effect.

Your patter could be soft and gentle; something like, "All right, little bunny, just relax now as I lay you on your back. With my right hand, I will separate your ears so they can rest on the table. Next I lay your legs on the table. And presto, you're asleep!"

Your patter could be more powerful and mysterious if you like. You might say, "And now watch carefully as I tame this angry lobster. As I stand him on his head, you'll notice that the mere touch of my fingers drains him of his fight. And now as I place one claw and then the other into position, he grows tamer yet. As I remove my hands, he will continue to stand on his head—and is completely in my power. The lobster is completely tame and will continue to stand on its head until I, Marvin the Magnificent, remove the spell!"

It's also fun to experiment with waking hypnosis. Remember, waking hypnosis is pure and simple suggestion and suggestion only. Concentration is necessary, but to a lesser degree than required by actual hypnosis. The biggest problem in successfully completing experiments in waking hypnosis, or suggestion, is to remain serious. Even the slightest smile can destroy the limited concentration that is necessary to success. It is also important to *believe* that the experiments will be successful. As you talk, your voice, your expression, even the way you hold your body, will influence the way your suggestions are received. Since trust is also a vital ingredient in these experiments, a good friend makes the best subject.

Barbara and Karen have decided to experiment with suggestion. Barbara will give the suggestions and Karen will accept them. They sit on the floor, facing each other. Barbara tells Karen to hold her hands out in front of her, palms up.

Now Barbara says, "Imagine that you're holding a big, heavy rock in your left hand. It's very, very heavy. It's so heavy that you wonder how long you'll be able to hold it up." She repeats similar suggestions until Karen's left hand begins to drop a little.

Next Barbara says, "Imagine a helium balloon tied to your right hand. It's lighter than air and it's pulling your right hand up into the air. The balloon is pulling your right hand higher and higher."

Once Karen's right hand begins to rise, Barbara switches back and forth between rock suggestions and balloon suggestions. All the while, Barbara keeps her voice a dull monotone and gazes into Karen's eyes.

As Barbara continues to give alternating suggestions, Karen is fascinated. She actually feels the weight in her left hand and the weightlessness in her right hand. Accordingly, her left hand

The power of suggestion — which hand is holding the balloon?
Which the rock?

falls slowly toward the ground while her right hand rises higher
and higher.

For the next experiment, both girls stand. Barbara stands
behind Karen and instructs her to choose something in front
of her to stare at.

Now Barbara suggests, "You are in a boat out on the water.
The waves rock the boat and you are beginning to sway back

and forth and back and forth. The waves are getting bigger and you're swaying farther forward and farther back each time the boat rocks. You love swaying with the waves." As Karen sways farther and farther, Barbara says, "You're swaying so far now that you wonder if you'll fall, but you're not worried about that because you know I'll catch you when you fall backward as the waves make the boat sway more and more."

Soon, Karen falls back into Barbara's waiting arms. Karen actually feels the waves controlling her movements as she hears Barbara's repeated suggestions.

The keys to success with any experiments in suggestion are to keep talking and to believe that the experiments *will* work. If you have any doubt, it will show in your voice and your manner, and the suggestions will be rejected. Also, be patient. It may take several minutes before your subject begins to accept your suggestions.

One final experiment can be done alone. It is perhaps the most fascinating of all because it is one way to get in touch with your own subconscious mind. All you need is a pendulum and a simple diagram.

To make a pendulum, take four or five inches of string or thread and tie a weight to one end. Just about any weight will do. It might be a ring or a safety pin or a fishing weight. As long as the weight is heavier than the string, the pendulum will work properly. A necklace with a pendant makes an excellent pendulum.

It's important to be serious as suggestions are repeated.

But you can't help a grin of amazement as you find yourself swaying and finally falling into the arms of your friend, who caused it all to happen with the power of suggestion.

Hold the pendulum between your thumb and forefinger and rest your elbow on a table in such a way that the weight dangles over the center point of a diagram like this one.

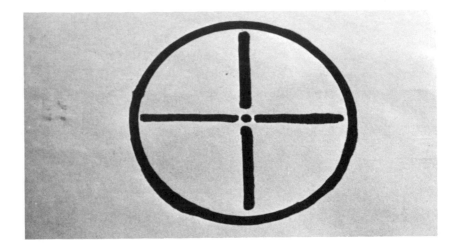

Begin by simply playing with the pendulum to get the feel of it. Move your fingers so that the pendulum begins to sway sideways back and forth along the line that crosses the circle. After the pendulum has begun to sway, stop moving your fingers and just let it sway by itself for a few moments.

Now move your fingers so that the pendulum begins to sway toward and away from you along the other line through the circle. Again, let it sway by itself for a few seconds.

Change the direction again so that the pendulum follows the circle around and around. And let it continue by itself.

The next step is to make the pendulum move in a certain direction by simply thinking of that direction. Keep your fingers still. Again, begin by dangling the pendulum over the center of the circle. Now begin to think, "The pendulum will begin to sway back and forth and back and forth . . ." Keep thinking this until the pendulum begins to move.

Just hold the pendulum and think about it starting to sway. Soon it will. It may move only a little at first, but as you continue to think about it swaying, it will go farther and farther until it follows the line on the diagram clear to the ends.

This may seem like magic, but it isn't. It is simply your subconscious mind telling your muscles to move.

The pendulum can move in four different directions. It can move sideways, it can go toward you and away, it can go clockwise, and it can go counterclockwise. Each of these directions can provide an answer to questions you might want to ask your subconscious mind. You can get, "Yes," "No," "I'm not sure," and "I don't want to answer." Ask your subconscious to choose a direction for each answer.

Rest your elbow on a table and dangle the pendulum over the center point of the diagram. Now ask, "Which direction will mean yes?" Continue repeating the question until the pendulum begins to move in a definite direction.

Without stopping the pendulum, say, "Now which direc-

The pendulum swings out.

tion means no?" Amazingly, the pendulum will slowly change its direction as you repeat this question. Continue like this until you know the direction for each answer.

Sometimes, the pendulum may move diagonally. This tells you that your question wasn't clear. You simply need to find a better way to ask it.

Many of the questions we ask and answer each day are not clear. "Will you tell me where you live?" is not a clear question. Does it mean, "Will you tell me?" or "Where do you

The pendulum swings sideways.

Dangle the pendulum over the circle's center point.

live?'' Your conscious mind would answer the question, "I live at 77 Hummingbird Lane." Your conscious mind has learned that when such a question is asked, what is meant is, "Where do you live?" not "Will you tell me?" But your subconscious mind would answer the question "Will you tell me?" with a yes or no. So be sure to ask the question you really want answered when you talk with your subconscious.

You can ask all sorts of questions from, "Do I really like Martha?" to "Can I learn to paint?" to "Do I really think I'm handsome?"

Using a pendulum to get in touch with the subconscious is both fun and interesting. We can learn a lot about ourselves in this way.

Suggested Reading

Anderson-Evangelista, Anita. *Hypnosis, A Journey into the Mind*. Arco Publishing, 1980.

Bernstein, Morey. *The Search for Bridey Murphey*. Doubleday, 1956.

Block, Eugene B. *Hypnosis, A New Tool in Crime Detection*. David McKay, 1976.

Clement, Pierre. *Hypnosis and Power Learning*. Westwood Publishing, 1979.

Cunningham, Les. *HypnoSport*. Westwood Publishing, 1981.

du Maurier, George. *Trilby*. Osgood, McIlvaine and Co., 1895, Unicorn, 1947.

Ehrenwald, Jan, M.D. *The ESP Experience — a Psychiatric Validation*. Basic Books, 1978.

Grass, Dean E. *The Learning Block*. Westwood Publishing, 1981.

Grossi, Ralph. *Reliving Reincarnation Through Hypnosis*. Exposition Press, 1975.

Hall, Elizabeth. *Possible Impossibilities*. Houghton Mifflin, 1977.

Hansel, C.E.M. *ESP and Parapsychology — A Critical Re-Evaluation*. Prometheus Books, 1980.

LeCron, Leslie M. *Self-Hypnotism: The Technique and Its Use in Daily Living.* Prentice-Hall, 1964.

McGill, Ormond. *Hypnotism and Meditation.* Westwood Publishing, 1981.

———. *Professional Stage Hypnotism.* Westwood Publishing, 1977.

Mutke, Peter H.C., M.D. *Selective Awareness.* Celestial Arts, 1976.

St. John, Adela Rogers. *No Good-Byes — My Search into Life Beyond Death.* McGraw-Hill Book Company, 1981.

Tebbetts, Charles. *Self-Hypnosis.* Westwood Publishing, 1977.

Index

About the Author

Born and raised in Washington State, VIVIAN KIRBY earned a bachelor's degree from the University of Washington in Seattle. She and her family make their home near Wenatchee, Washington where they operate a large cherry and apple orchard. Mrs. Kirby works at writing and home-making as well as helping with the orchard business. She has been interested in and has done research in hypnosis for a number of years.